TABLE OF CONTENTS

This guide provides an overview of Federal civil rights laws that ensure equal opportunity for people with disabilities. To find out more about how these laws may apply to you, contact the agencies and organizations listed below.

Americans with Disabilities Act (ADA)

The ADA prohibits discrimination on the basis of disability in employment, State and local government, public accommodations, commercial facilities, transportation, and telecommunications. It also applies to the United States Congress.

To be protected by the ADA, one must have a disability or have a relationship or association with an individual with a disability. An individual with a disability is defined by the ADA as a person who has a physical or mental impairment that substantially limits one or more major life activities, a person who has a history or record of such an impairment, or a person who is perceived by others as having such an impairment. The ADA does not specifically name all of the impairments that are covered.

ADA Title I: Employment

Title I requires employers with 15 or more employees to provide qualified individuals with disabilities an equal opportunity to benefit from the full range of employment-related opportunities available to others. For example, it prohibits discrimination in recruitment, hiring, promotions, training, pay, social activities, and other privileges of employment. It restricts questions that can be asked about an applicant's disability before a job offer is made, and it requires that employers make reasonable accommodation to the known physical or mental limitations of otherwise qualified individuals with disabilities, unless it results in undue hardship. Religious entities with 15 or more employees are covered under title I.

Title I complaints must be filed with the U. S. Equal Employment Opportunity Commission (EEOC) within 180 days of the date of discrimination, or 300 days if the charge is filed with a designated State or local fair employment practice agency. Individuals may file a lawsuit in Federal court only after they receive a "right-to-sue" letter from the EEOC.

Charges of employment discrimination on the basis of disability may be filed at any U.S. Equal Employment Opportunity Commission field office. Field offices are located in 50 cities throughout the U.S. and are listed in most telephone directories under "U.S. Government." For the appropriate EEOC field office in your geographic area, contact:

> (800) 669-4000 (voice)
> (800) 669-6820 (TTY)
>
> www.eeoc.gov

Publications and information on EEOC-enforced laws may be obtained by calling:

> (800) 669-3362 (voice)
> (800) 800-3302 (TTY)

For information on how to accommodate a specific individual with a disability, contact the Job Accommodation Network at:

> (800) 526-7234 (voice)
> (800) 781-9403 (TTY)
>
> http://askjan.org

ADA Title II: State and Local Government Activities

Title II covers all activities of State and local governments regardless of the government entity's size or receipt of Federal funding. Title II requires that State and local governments give people with disabilities an equal opportunity to benefit from all of their programs, services, and activities (e.g. public education, employment, transportation, recreation, health care, social services, courts, voting, and town meetings).

State and local governments are required to follow specific architectural standards in the new construction and alteration of their buildings. They also must relocate programs or otherwise provide access in inaccessible older buildings, and communicate effectively with people who have hearing, vision, or speech disabilities. Public entities are not required to take actions that would result in undue financial and administrative burdens. They are required to make reasonable modifications to policies, practices, and procedures where necessary to avoid discrimination, unless they can demonstrate that doing so would fundamentally alter the nature of the service, program, or activity being provided.

Complaints of title II violations may be filed with the Department of Justice within 180 days of the date of discrimination. In certain situations, cases may be referred to a mediation program sponsored by the Department. The Department may bring a lawsuit where it has investigated a matter and has been unable to resolve violations. For more information, contact:

> U.S. Department of Justice
> Civil Rights Division
> 950 Pennsylvania Avenue, N.W.
> Disability Rights Section - NYAV
> Washington, D.C. 20530
>
> www.ada.gov
>
> (800) 514-0301 (voice)
> (800) 514-0383 (TTY)

Title II may also be enforced through private lawsuits in Federal court. It is not necessary to file a complaint with the Department of Justice (DOJ) or any other Federal agency, or to receive a "right-to-sue" letter, before going to court.

ADA Title II: Public Transportation

The transportation provisions of title II cover public transportation services, such as city buses and public rail transit (e.g. subways, commuter rails, Amtrak). Public transportation authorities may not discriminate against people with disabilities in the provision of their services. They must comply with requirements for accessibility in newly purchased vehicles, make good faith efforts to purchase or lease accessible used buses, remanufacture buses in an accessible manner, and, unless it would result in an undue burden, provide paratransit where they operate fixed-route bus or rail systems. Paratransit is a service where individuals who are unable to use the regular transit system independently (because of a physical or mental impairment) are picked up and dropped off at their destinations. Questions and complaints about public transportation should be directed to:

Office of Civil Rights
Federal Transit Administration U.S.
Department of Transportation
1200 New Jersey Avenue, S.E.
Room E 54 - 427
Washington, D.C. 20590

www.fta.dot.gov/ada

(888) 446-4511 (voice/relay)

ADA Title III: Public Accommodations

Title III covers businesses and nonprofit service providers that are public accommodations, privately operated entities offering certain types of courses and examinations, privately operated transportation, and commercial facilities. Public accommodations are private entities who own, lease, lease to, or operate facilities such as restaurants, retail stores, hotels, movie theaters, private schools, convention centers, doctors' offices, homeless shelters, transportation depots, zoos, funeral homes, day care centers, and recreation facilities including sports stadiums and fitness clubs. Transportation services provided by private entities are also covered by title III.

Public accommodations must comply with basic nondiscrimination requirements that prohibit exclusion, segregation, and unequal treatment. They also must comply with specific requirements related to architectural standards for new and altered buildings; reasonable modifications to policies, practices, and procedures; effective communication with people with hearing, vision, or speech disabilities; and other access requirements. Additionally, public accommodations must remove barriers in existing buildings where it is easy to do so without much difficulty or expense, given the public accommodation's resources.

Courses and examinations related to professional, educational, or trade-related applications, licensing, certifications, or credentialing must be provided in a place and manner accessible to people with disabilities, or alternative accessible arrangements must be offered.

Commercial facilities, such as factories and warehouses, must comply with the ADA's architectural standards for new construction and alterations.

Complaints of title III violations may be filed with the Department of Justice. In certain situations, cases may be referred to a mediation program sponsored by the Department. The Department is authorized to bring a lawsuit where there is a pattern or practice of discrimination in violation of title III, or where an act of discrimination raises an issue of general public importance. Title III may also be enforced through private lawsuits. It is not necessary to file a complaint with the Department of Justice (or any Federal agency), or to receive a "right-to-sue" letter, before going to court. For more information, contact:

> U.S. Department of Justice
> Civil Rights Division
> 950 Pennsylvania Avenue, N.W.
> Disability Rights Section - NYAV
> Washington, D.C. 20530
>
> www.ada.gov
>
> (800) 514-0301 (voice)
> (800) 514-0383 (TTY)

ADA Title IV: Telecommunications Relay Services

    Title IV addresses telephone and television access for people with hearing and speech disabilities. It requires common carriers (telephone companies) to establish interstate and intrastate telecommunications relay services (TRS) 24 hours a day, 7 days a week. TRS enables callers with hearing and speech disabilities who use TTYs (also known as TDDs), and callers who use voice telephones to communicate with each other through a third party communications assistant. The Federal Communications Commission (FCC) has set minimum standards for TRS services. Title IV also requires closed captioning of Federally funded public service announcements. For more information about TRS, contact the FCC at:

                Federal Communications Commission
                445 12th Street, S.W.
                Washington, D.C. 20554

                www.fcc.gov/cgb/dro

                (888) 225-5322 (Voice)
                (888) 835-5322 (TTY)

Telecommunications Act

Section 255 and Section 251(a)(2) of the Communications Act of 1934, as amended by the Telecommunications Act of 1996, require manufacturers of telecommunications equipment and providers of telecommunications services to ensure that such equipment and services are accessible to and usable by persons with disabilities, if readily achievable. These amendments ensure that people with disabilities will have access to a broad range of products and services such as telephones, cell phones, pagers, call-waiting, and operator services, that were often inaccessible to many users with disabilities. For more information, contact:

Federal Communications Commission
445 12th Street, S.W.
Washington, D.C. 20554

www.fcc.gov/cgb/dro

(888) 225-5322 (Voice)
(888) 835-5322 (TTY)

Fair Housing Act

The Fair Housing Act, as amended in 1988, prohibits housing discrimination on the basis of race, color, religion, sex, disability, familial status, and national origin. Its coverage includes private housing, housing that receives Federal financial assistance, and State and local government housing. It is unlawful to discriminate in any aspect of selling or renting housing or to deny a dwelling to a buyer or renter because of the disability of that individual, an individual associated with the buyer or renter, or an individual who intends to live in the residence. Other covered activities include, for example, financing, zoning practices, new construction design, and advertising.

The Fair Housing Act requires owners of housing facilities to make reasonable exceptions in their policies and operations to afford people with disabilities equal housing opportunities. For example, a landlord with a "no pets" policy may be required to grant an exception to this rule and allow an individual who is blind to keep a guide dog in the residence. The Fair Housing Act also requires landlords to allow tenants with disabilities to make reasonable access-related modifications to their private living space, as well as to common use spaces. (The landlord is not required to pay for the changes.) The Act further requires that new multifamily housing with four or more units be designed and built to allow access for persons with disabilities. This includes accessible common use areas, doors that are wide enough for wheelchairs, kitchens and bathrooms that allow a person using a wheelchair to maneuver, and other adaptable features within the units.

Complaints of Fair Housing Act violations may be filed with the U.S. Department of Housing and Urban Development. For more information or to file a complaint, contact:

> Office of Compliance and Disability Rights Division
> Office of Fair Housing and Equal Opportunity
> U.S. Department of Housing and Urban Development
> 451 7th Street, S.W., Room 5242
> Washington, D.C. 20410
>
> www.hud.gov/offices/fheo
>
> (800) 669-9777 (voice)
> (800) 927-9275 (TTY)

For questions about the accessibility provisions of the Fair Housing Act, you may contact Fair Housing Accessibility FIRST at:

> www.fairhousingfirst.org
>
> (888) 341-7781 (voice/TTY)

For publications, you may call the Housing and Urban Development Customer Service Center at:

> (800) 767-7468 (voice/relay)

Additionally, the Department of Justice can file cases involving a pattern or practice of discrimination. The Fair Housing Act may also be enforced through private lawsuits.

Air Carrier Access Act

The Air Carrier Access Act prohibits discrimination in air transportation by domestic and foreign air carriers against qualified individuals with physical or mental impairments. It applies only to air carriers that provide regularly scheduled services for hire to the public. Requirements address a wide range of issues including boarding assistance and certain accessibility features in newly built aircraft and new or altered airport facilities. People may enforce rights under the Air Carrier Access Act by filing a complaint with the U.S. Department of Transportation, or by bringing a lawsuit in Federal court. For more information or to file a complaint, contact:

> Aviation Consumer Protection Division, C-75
> U.S. Department of Transportation
> 1200 New Jersey Avenue, S.E.
> Washington, D.C. 20590
>
> http://airconsumer.ost.dot.gov
>
> (202) 366-2220 (voice)
> (202) 366-0511 (TTY)
>
> (800) 778-4838 (voice)
> (800) 455-9880 (TTY)

Voting Accessibility for the Elderly and Handicapped Act

The Voting Accessibility for the Elderly and Handicapped Act of 1984 generally requires polling places across the United States to be physically accessible to people with disabilities for federal elections. Where no accessible location is available to serve as a polling place, a political subdivision must provide an alternate means of casting a ballot on the day of the election. This law also requires states to make available registration and voting aids for disabled and elderly voters, including information by TTYs (also known as TDDs) or similar devices. For more information, contact:

U.S. Department of Justice
Civil Rights Division
950 Pennsylvania Avenue, N.W.
Voting Section - 1800G
Washington, D.C. 20530

(800) 253-3931 (voice/TTY)

National Voter Registration Act

The National Voter Registration Act of 1993, also known as the "Motor Voter Act," makes it easier for all Americans to exercise their fundamental right to vote. One of the basic purposes of the Act is to increase the historically low registration rates of minorities and persons with disabilities that have resulted from discrimination. The Motor Voter Act requires all offices of State-funded programs that are primarily engaged in providing services to persons with disabilities to provide all program applicants with voter registration forms, to assist them in completing the forms, and to transmit completed forms to the appropriate State official. For more information, contact:

U.S. Department of Justice
Civil Rights Division
950 Pennsylvania Avenue, N.W.
Voting Section - 1800G
Washington, D.C. 20530

www.usdoj.gov/crt/voting

(800) 253-3931 (voice/TTY)

Civil Rights of Institutionalized Persons Act

The Civil Rights of Institutionalized Persons Act (CRIPA) authorizes the U.S. Attorney General to investigate conditions of confinement at State and local government institutions such as prisons, jails, pretrial detention centers, juvenile correctional facilities, publicly operated nursing homes, and institutions for people with psychiatric or developmental disabilities. Its purpose is to allow the Attorney General to uncover and correct widespread deficiencies that seriously jeopardize the health and safety of residents of institutions. The Attorney General does not have authority under CRIPA to investigate isolated incidents or to represent individual institutionalized persons.

The Attorney General may initiate civil law suits where there is reasonable cause to believe that conditions are "egregious or flagrant," that they are subjecting residents to "grievous harm," and that they are part of a "pattern or practice" of resistance to residents' full enjoyment of constitutional or Federal rights, including title II of the ADA and section 504 of the Rehabilitation Act. For more information or to bring a matter to the Department of Justice's attention, contact:

U.S. Department of Justice
Civil Rights Division
950 Pennsylvania Avenue, N.W.
Special Litigation Section - PHB
Washington, D.C. 20530

www.usdoj.gov/crt/split

(877) 218-5228 (voice/TTY)

Individuals with Disabilities Education Act

The Individuals with Disabilities Education Act (IDEA) (formerly called P.L. 94-142 or the Education for all Handicapped Children Act of 1975) requires public schools to make available to all eligible children with disabilities a free appropriate public education in the least restrictive environment appropriate to their individual needs.

IDEA requires public school systems to develop appropriate Individualized Education Programs (IEP's) for each child. The specific special education and related services outlined in each IEP reflect the individualized needs of each student.

IDEA also mandates that particular procedures be followed in the development of the IEP. Each student's IEP must be developed by a team of knowledgeable persons and must be at least reviewed annually. The team includes the child's teacher; the parents, subject to certain limited exceptions; the child, if determined appropriate; an agency representative who is qualified to provide or supervise the provision of special education; and other individuals at the parents' or agency's discretion.

If parents disagree with the proposed IEP, they can request a due process hearing and a review from the State educational agency if applicable in that state. They also can appeal the State agency's decision to State or Federal court. For more information, contact:

Office of Special Education & Rehabilitative Services
U.S. Department of Education
400 Maryland Avenue, S.W.
Washington, D.C. 20202-7100

www.ed.gov/about/offices/list/osers/osep

(202) 245-7468 (voice/TTY)

Rehabilitation Act

The Rehabilitation Act prohibits discrimination on the basis of disability in programs conducted by Federal agencies, in programs receiving Federal financial assistance, in Federal employment, and in the employment practices of Federal contractors. The standards for determining employment discrimination under the Rehabilitation Act are the same as those used in title I of the Americans with Disabilities Act.

Section 501

Section 501 requires affirmative action and nondiscrimination in employment by Federal agencies of the executive branch. To obtain more information or to file a complaint, employees should contact their agency's Equal Employment Opportunity Office.

Section 503

Section 503 requires affirmative action and prohibits employment discrimination by Federal government contractors and subcontractors with contracts of more than $10,000. For more information on section 503, contact:

Office of Federal Contract Compliance Programs
U.S. Department of Labor
200 Constitution Avenue, N.W., Room C-3325
Washington, D.C. 20210

www.dol.gov/ofccp/index.htm

(202) 693-0106 (voice/relay)

Section 504

Section 504 states that "no qualified individual with a disability in the United States shall be excluded from, denied the benefits of, or be subjected to discrimination under" any program or activity that either receives Federal financial assistance or is conducted by any Executive agency or the United States Postal Service.

Each Federal agency has its own set of section 504 regulations that apply to its own programs. Agencies that provide Federal financial assistance also have section 504 regulations covering entities that receive Federal aid. Requirements common to these regulations include reasonable accommodation for employees with disabilities; program accessibility; effective communication with people who have hearing or vision disabilities; and accessible new construction and alterations. Each agency is responsible for enforcing its own regulations. Section 504 may also be enforced through private lawsuits. It is not necessary to file a complaint with a Federal agency or to receive a "right-to-sue" letter before going to court.

For information on how to file 504 complaints with the appropriate agency, contact:

U.S. Department of Justice
Civil Rights Division
950 Pennsylvania Avenue, N.W.
Disability Rights Section - NYAV
Washington, D.C. 20530

www.ada.gov

(800) 514-0301 (voice)
(800) 514-0383 (TTY)

Section 508

Section 508 establishes requirements for electronic and information technology developed, maintained, procured, or used by the Federal government. Section 508 requires Federal electronic and information technology to be accessible to people with disabilities, including employees and members of the public.

An accessible information technology system is one that can be operated in a variety of ways and does not rely on a single sense or ability of the user. For example, a system that provides output only in visual format may not be accessible to people with visual impairments and a system that provides output only in audio format may not be accessible to people who are deaf or hard of hearing. Some individuals with disabilities may need accessibility-related software or peripheral devices in order to use systems that comply with Section 508. For more information on section 508, contact:

U.S. General Services Administration
Office of Government-wide Policy
IT Accessibility & Workforce Division (ITAW)
1800 F Street, N.W.
Room 2222, MEC:ITAW
Washington, DC 20405-0001

www.gsa.gov/portal/content/105254

(202) 501-4906 (voice)

U.S. Architectural and Transportation
Barriers Compliance Board
1331 F Street, N.W., Suite 1000
Washington, DC 20004-1111

www.access-board.gov

800-872-2253 (voice)
800-993-2822 (TTY)

Architectural Barriers Act

The Architectural Barriers Act (ABA) requires that buildings and facilities that are designed, constructed, or altered with Federal funds, or leased by a Federal agency, comply with Federal standards for physical accessibility. ABA requirements are limited to architectural standards in new and altered buildings and in newly leased facilities. They do not address the activities conducted in those buildings and facilities. Facilities of the U.S. Postal Service are covered by the ABA. For more information or to file a complaint, contact:

U.S. Architectural and Transportation
Barriers Compliance Board
1331 F Street, N.W., Suite 1000
Washington, D.C. 20004-1111

www.access-board.gov

(800) 872-2253 (voice)
(800) 993-2822 (TTY)

General Sources of Disability Rights Information

ADA Information Line
(800) 514-0301 (voice)
(800) 514-0383 (TTY)
www.ada.gov

Regional Disability and Business
Technical Assistance Centers
(800) 949-4232 (voice/TTY)
www.adata.org

Statute Citations

Air Carrier Access Act of 1986
49 U.S.C. § 41705
  ImplementingRegulation:
    14 CFR Part 382

Americans with Disabilities Act of 1990
42 U.S.C. §§ 12101 et seq.
  ImplementingRegulations:
    29 CFR Parts 1630, 1602 (Title I, EEOC)
    28 CFR Part 35 (Title II, Department of Justice)
    49 CFR Parts 27, 37, 38 (Title II, III, Department
      of Transportation)
    28 CFR Part 36 (Title III, Department of Justice)
    47 CFR §§ 64.601 et seq. (Title IV, FCC)

Architectural Barriers Act of 1968
42 U.S.C. §§ 4151 et seq.
  ImplementingRegulation:
    41 CFR Subpart 101-19.6

Civil Rights of Institutionalized Persons Act
42 U.S.C. §§ 1997 et seq.

Fair Housing Amendments Act of 1988
42 U.S.C. §§ 3601 et seq.
  ImplementingRegulation:
    24 CFR Parts 100 et seq.

Individuals with Disabilities Education Act
20 U.S.C. §§ 1400 et seq.
  ImplementingRegulation:
    34 CFR Part 300

National Voter Registration Act of 1993
42 U.S.C. §§ 1973gg et seq.

Section 501 of the Rehabilitation Act of 1973, as amended
29 U.S.C. § 791
  Implementing Regulation:
    29 CFR § 1614.203

Section 503 of the Rehabilitation Act of 1973, as amended
29 U.S.C. § 793
  Implementing Regulation:
    41 CFR Part 60-741

Section 504 of the Rehabilitation Act of 1973, as amended
29 U.S.C. § 794

Over 20 Implementing Regulations for federally assisted
programs, including:
    34 CFR Part 104 (Department of Education)
    45 CFR Part 84 (Department of Health and
      Human Services)
    28 CFR §§ 42.501 et seq.

Over 95 Implementing Regulations for federally conducted
programs, including:
    28 CFR Part 39 (Department of Justice)

Section 508 of the Rehabilitation Act of 1973, as amended
29 U.S.C. § 794d

Telecommunications Act of 1996
47 U.S.C. §§ 255, 251(a)(2)

**Voting Accessibility for the Elderly and Handicapped Act
of 1984**
42 U.S.C. §§ 1973ee et seq.

www.ingramcontent.com/pod-product-compliance
Lightning Source LLC
Chambersburg PA
CBHW051424170526
45165CB00004BA/1949